P9-DGE-618

Rookie
Read-About® Science

The Moon

By Carmen Bredeson

Consultants

Orsola De Marco, Ph.D.
Department of Astrophysics
American Museum of Natural History
New York, New York

Jeanne Clidas, Ph.D.
National Literacy Consultant

Katy Kane
Educational Consultant

CP Children's Press®
A Division of Scholastic Inc.
New York   Toronto   London   Auckland   Sydney
Mexico City   New Delhi   Hong Kong
Danbury, Connecticut

Designer: Herman Adler Design
Photo Researcher: Caroline Anderson
The photo on the cover shows the Moon.

Library of Congress Cataloging-in-Publication Data

Bredeson, Carmen.
    The moon / by Carmen Bredeson.
        p. cm.
Summary: A simple introduction to the physical features, orbit, and
efforts to explore the Earth's moon.
    ISBN 0-516-22864-1 (lib. bdg.)   0-516-27770-7 (pbk.)
    1. Moon—Juvenile literature. [1. Moon.] I. Title.
    QB582 .B74 2003
    523.3—dc21
                                        2002011216

What are those dark areas
that make the moon look
like a face?

A volcano on Earth

They are pools of hard lava. Long ago, hot lava gushed out of volcanoes on the Moon. It cooled and became hard.

From Earth, the dark lava looks like the "Man in the Moon."

The Moon was probably
once a part of Earth.

A huge rock from space
hit Earth four billion years
ago. It blasted off chunks
that became the Moon.

8

The Moon has many
big holes called craters
(CRAY-turs).

Space rocks make craters
when they crash into
the Moon.

Most of the craters are
very old.

The Moon is about one-fourth the size of Earth.

Imagine cutting Earth into four pieces. The Moon would be the size of one of those pieces.

11

The Moon does not have any light of its own. It reflects light from the Sun like a mirror reflects light.

The Moon goes all the way around Earth every four weeks.

During its trip, different parts of the Moon reflect sunlight toward Earth.

That is why the Moon
seems to change shape.

The amount of the Moon
that we see changes.

Sometimes the Sun shines
on the whole side of the
Moon that faces Earth.
Then we see a full moon.

Sometimes we see only
a quarter of the Moon.

Other times we see just a
tiny sliver, called a crescent
(KRESS-uhnt).

Sometimes we see no
moon at all.

We saw the Moon up
close for the first time
in 1969. That is when
astronauts landed there.
We saw the landing
on television.

The astronauts had to wear big space suits and tanks of air. There is no air to breathe on the Moon.

Twelve astronauts have
walked on the Moon.
They brought 800 pounds
of Moon rocks home
to Earth.

Scientists study the rocks
to learn about the Moon.

Would you like to touch a Moon rock? You can touch one at museums in Texas, Florida, and Washington, D.C.

Imagine sliding your fingers across a real piece of the Moon!

Words You Know

astronaut

crater

crescent

full moon

space suit

volcano

31

Index

About the Author

Carmen Bredeson has written dozens of nonfiction books for children. She lives in Texas and enjoys traveling and doing research for her books.

Photo Credits